T11508

DERBYSHIRE
COUNTY LIBRARY

Date 2 0 AUG 1993

Class ....

SCHOOL LIBRARY SERVICE

SAINT BENEDICT SCHOOL
DUFFIELD ROAD
DERBY DE22 1JD

KU-685-286

SPEED

BRENDA WALPOLE

Photographs by Chris Fairclough
Illustrations by Dennis Tinkler

Contents

A & C Black · London

Hurry up! Get a move on!

Over the centuries, people have dreamed of being able to travel faster and faster. In ancient legends, many of the gods were famous for their speed. Hermes, the Greek messenger of the gods had wings on his heels, and the Nordic god, Thor, sped across the sky in his chariot so fast that he made claps of thunder.

Why is it important to measure speed?

Car drivers may need to know how long a journey is going to take. They should also drive at the correct speed for safety.

When you've judged the speed of a ball you can move into place to catch it.

Measuring the speed of someone's heart beat is one way to check that they are healthy.

Can you think of any other reasons why we need to measure speed?

Every time we take a measurement of speed, we need to know two things: what has happened and the time it has taken. A doctor listens to the number of times your heart beats per minute. This is called your heart rate. To measure how fast something is moving we need to know the distance it has travelled and the time the journey has taken. We measure the speed of a car in kilometres per hour or miles per hour.

Speed on land

To prehistoric people, speed was important for hunting and escaping from enemies. Those who could run the fastest were more likely to survive.

Thousands of years ago, great sporting events were organised, in which runners competed against each other. This ancient Greek vase shows some long distance runners. In 776 BC, in ancient Greece, the first Olympic Games were held. At these games the fastest runners were heroes. In 490 BC, an army messenger ran approximately 40 kilometres from a battle at Marathon to Athens, where he reported a victory. Today athletes run in a long distance race called a marathon.

Even when things travel for just a few seconds or minutes, we sometimes give their speeds in kilometres per hour or miles per hour. The fastest human sprinters can run at speeds of 40 kilometres per hour. The fastest animal is the cheetah which can reach speeds of 100 kilometres per hour. But neither the sprinter nor the cheetah can keep up these speeds for long. Often, a cheetah fails to catch prey, such as antelope, because although an antelope is slower than a cheetah it can keep going for longer.

Something to try

Find out how fast you walk

You will need: a measuring stick or a tape measure, and a stopwatch or a watch with a second hand.

Pace out a distance of 100 metres, or use a running track or sports field. For exactly 5 minutes walk up and down the track at a speed which is comfortable for you. Keep note of how many metres you have walked. Work out how many metres you would travel in one hour if you kept up the same speed. How many kilometres per hour is this? (If you need more help with this see page 31.)

The slowest mammal is the three-toed sloth which travels at only 2.4 metres per minute.

5

To calculate walking and running speeds or the speed of a car, the time is measured in minutes or hours and the distance in metres and kilometres. Rockets and satellites move so quickly they travel thousands of kilometres in one hour. Often, their speeds are recorded in kilometres per second. Which units would you use to measure the speed of a snail?

Every car has a speedometer to show the driver how fast the car is moving. The pointer on the speedometer's dial is connected to the car's engine by a flexible cable. When the driver presses the accelerator, the engine makes the wheels turn faster and cover more ground. The distance travelled by the wheels is converted into kilometres or miles per hour and shown on the speedometer.

The land speed record is the speed of the fastest car in the world, 1019.467 kilometres per hour, set by Richard Noble in 1983, driving Thrust 2.

Measuring speed in sport

In sporting events, when athletes race over a set distance, electronic timing devices are often used to record the speed of the competitors. Sometimes the judges use photographs of the athletes as they cross the finishing-line to help them decide who has won.

In downhill ski races, each skier passes through light beams at the start-gate which trigger a timing mechanism. These beams are linked to the control room and a digital display-timer, which is accurate to one hundredth of a second. At the finishing-line, the skier passes through another beam of light to stop the clock.

Speed on water

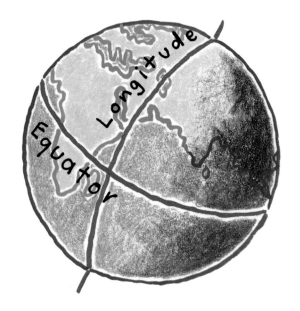

The speed of a ship is measured in knots. A ship travelling at one knot covers a distance of one nautical mile per hour. A nautical mile (1,852 metres) is longer than a land mile (1,604 metres). A nautical mile is a special measure of distance used in the air and on water. It is calculated from a tiny part of the distance of a Great Circle, which is a complete circle round the Earth such as the equator or a line of longitude.

Hundreds of years ago, a ship's speed was measured with a log-line. This was a wooden log attached to a length of rope which was knotted at measured intervals. The rope measured 150 fathoms. A fathom is 1.82 metres. The rope was wound round a reel on the ship and the log was thrown overboard. As the ship moved forward the rope unwound. The number of knots that passed through a sailor's hands in a measured period of time was the ship's speed in knots. The ship's speed was written in a book called the ship's log-book.

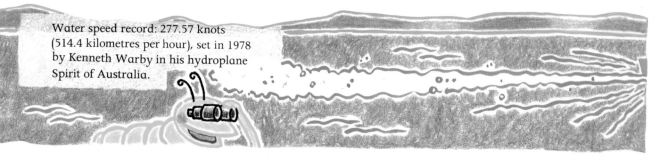

Water speed record: 277.57 knots (514.4 kilometres per hour), set in 1978 by Kenneth Warby in his hydroplane Spirit of Australia.

Make your own log-line for a toy boat

You will need: a toy boat, a pencil, which fits loosely inside a cotton reel, fine string or thread, a short twig, sellotape, plasticine, a tank or bath of water.

Tie knots in the thread at intervals of about 10 centimetres. Tape one end of the thread to the cotton reel and wind the rest round the reel. Tie the twig to the free end of the thread. Feed the pencil through the middle of the reel and press on to blobs of plasticine on the sides of the boat. Make sure the reel can turn freely. Float the twig on the water and gently push the boat forward. As the reel turns, count how many knots unwind. If you live near a pond where you can float your boat safely, try to find out the speed of the boat in knots per minute.

Speed in the air

Planes have to take off and cruise at certain speeds, otherwise they are pulled back to Earth by the force of gravity. Pilots keep a close check on their aircraft using instruments that measure the speed of the plane as it flies through the air. This is called air speed and is measured differently from speed on the ground.

A plane's speed depends on the power of its engines, which give it thrust to move forward and to overcome air resistance which drags it back. Speeding forward gives the plane lift and allows the plane to take off and climb into the sky. If the plane flies too slowly, it will stall and quickly begin to fall.

Watch the flight path of a paper dart

Throw the dart forward as hard as you can so that the dart flies at speed. How far does it fly before it falls? Throw the dart again with less force so that it flies slowly. How far does it fly this time? Watch the dart's flight path and note its speed when it stalls and falls to the ground. Can you think of any other reasons why the dart might stall?

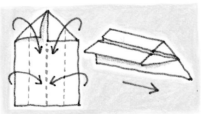

All aircraft are fitted with an air speed measurer called a Pitot tube, named after the eighteenth century scientist Henri Pitot. As the plane moves forward, the Pitot tube measures the pressure of air rushing into the tube. This information is fed into a computer in the cockpit and shown on a dial as the speed of the plane.

In 1988, Concorde flew from London to New York in the record time of 2 hours 55 minutes 15 seconds.

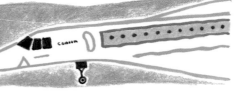

As fast as the wind

The direction and strength of the wind are important to pilots because they affect the speed of the planes. At airports, pilots look at windsocks to estimate the strength of the wind and to see in which direction it's blowing.

Something to try

Make your own windsock

You will need: a bamboo cane, an old pair of tights or socks, thin wire, sellotape or a stapler, scissors.

Cut the toes from one foot of the tights and make hoops of wire for each end. On one hoop leave a length of wire to push down the middle of the cane. Fold one edge of tight round the wire and staple or tape in place. Do the same at the other end. Take the windsock outdoors and stick it in some earth or hold it upright.

As the wind blows, the sock fills with air and points in the direction the wind is blowing. If the sock blows out stiffly, the wind is strong. If it hangs loosely, the wind is light.

Meteorologists study the weather. They use anemometers to record the speed of the wind.

Something to try

Make an anemometer to see how fast the wind blows

You will need: four paper cups, sellotape, two lengths of soft dowelling 20 centimetres long, a flat piece of wood for a plinth, stones, a dress pin, scissors, a small bead.

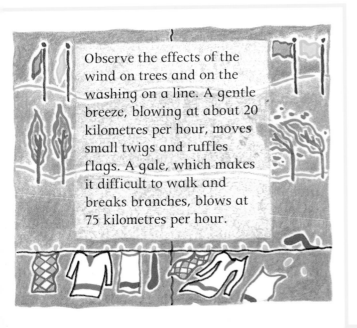

Observe the effects of the wind on trees and on the washing on a line. A gentle breeze, blowing at about 20 kilometres per hour, moves small twigs and ruffles flags. A gale, which makes it difficult to walk and breaks branches, blows at 75 kilometres per hour.

Tape the lengths of dowelling into a cross. Cut slits in the cups and push them on to the ends of the cross, top to tail so they make a circle. Push a pin through the middle of the cross, then through the bead and into the pole. The cross should be able to spin freely. Attach the pole to the plinth. Take your anemometer outside. What happens when there is a gust of wind?

P.S. Find out about Admiral Sir Francis Beaufort and the scale he invented for judging the speed of the wind.

13

Speeding up and slowing down

On Earth, any machine or living thing needs energy to make it move. You get the energy you need from the food you eat and from oxygen in the air. The food and oxygen are fuel, rather like the petrol which a car needs to make it go. Food and oxygen are carried in your blood, which is pumped round your body by your heart. When you exercise, your heart rate and breathing rate speed up to keep your muscles supplied with the fuel they need.

Something to try

See how your heart rate speeds up

Feel the pulse in your wrist with your fingers and count how many times it beats per minute. Now skip for 5 minutes and take your pulse again. Rest for a few minutes then walk at a brisk pace for 5 minutes and take your pulse again. Record your results on a chart.

14

P.S. Do you think your results would be different if you didn't take a rest between activities?

When a car driver presses the accelerator pedal, the car's engine receives more fuel and the car speeds up. Cars carry a reserve of stored energy in the petrol tank. If the car runs out of petrol, it slows down and stops.

Something to try

Make a toy with a reserve of energy wound up in a rubber band

You will need: a plastic bottle, a rubber band, some small pieces of dowelling, scissors, a bead, a thin piece of wire.

Make a hole in the base of the bottle and thread the rubber band through. Hold the loop in place with a piece of dowelling. Fish out the other end of the band with a wire hook. Thread the rubber band through the bead, which should just fit the neck of the bottle. Hold the loop in place with the dowelling; this is the propeller. Turn the propeller round so it twists the rubber band. Place the bottle on its side and let the propeller go. What happens when the rubber band unwinds?

Friction

On Earth, anything which moves uses some energy to overcome the force friction, which slows down moving objects. Friction is caused whenever one moving surface touches another. Objects move fastest on smooth surfaces. You can skate easily on ice but not on a concrete path. Objects grip on to rough surfaces which cause more friction than smooth ones.

Make your own speed test

You will need: a large board, some books, a crayon, a rubber, a coin, a stone, a cotton reel, a piece of sandpaper.

Prop up one end of the board on some books. Hold the objects at the top of the board and let them all go at the same time. Which object reaches the bottom first? Cover the board with a piece of sandpaper and try the test again. Which surface causes less friction? Can you think how you might speed up the objects?

P.S. Change the angle of the slope of the board and repeat the test. What happens?

16

Friction can be reduced by making surfaces smooth and even. When we want things to move at great speed, such as ice-skates or a toboggan, we polish and shine them. Another way to reduce friction is to separate the surfaces with a thin layer of liquid, called a lubricant. The thin layer of melted ice under an ice-skate makes it travel even faster. You travel much faster down a water slide than down an ordinary one because the water acts as a lubricant.

Oil is a lubricant which is often used in machines with moving parts. As a machine works, the moving parts rub against one another. This slows things down and the parts begin to wear. Oil helps the parts move faster and stops them from wearing out so quickly.

P.S. Lubricate the board with a little washing-up liquid and try the speed test again. What happens?

SAINT BENEDICT SCHOOL
DUFFIELD ROAD
DERBY. DE22 1JD

Wheeling along

When you want to move an object from one place to another, carrying or dragging it along the ground is slow, hard work. It's quicker and easier to move things on rollers, which keep the object off the ground. The huge stones used to build the pyramids were probably moved on rollers. Today, we still use rollers to help move goods more easily. Can you think where?

Something to try

Make your own rollers

You will need: some cotton reels and a big heavy book or object.

Place the cotton reels on the table and put the book on top. Push the book forward with your hand. Can you discover any problems using rollers?

Usually, wheels are better than rollers because they remain fixed to their load. No one knows exactly who invented the wheel, but in 3000 BC in Mesopotamia, solid wheels joined to a pole, called an axle, were being used. In about 1750 BC, wheels with spokes were first used in Egypt. These are lighter than solid wheels, which meant that vehicles could move more easily.

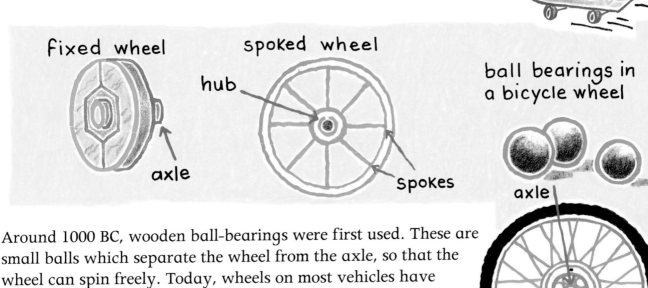

fixed wheel

spoked wheel

hub

axle

spokes

ball bearings in a bicycle wheel

axle

Around 1000 BC, wooden ball-bearings were first used. These are small balls which separate the wheel from the axle, so that the wheel can spin freely. Today, wheels on most vehicles have steel ball bearings.

Something to try

Make your own ball bearings

You will need: two syrup tins, or tins with lever-off lids, a few marbles.

Rest one tin upside down on top of the other and try to spin the top one round. Arrange a few marbles round the rim of the bottom tin and repeat the test. What happens?

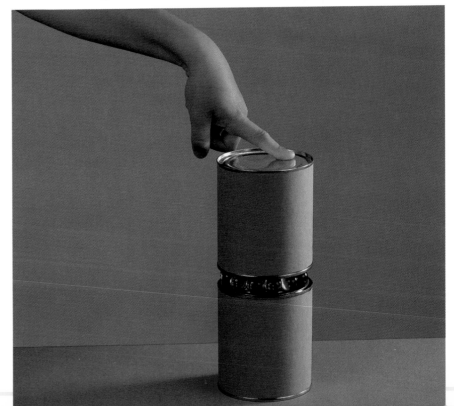

Friction can be useful when it stops things from travelling too quickly. Brakes on a bicycle press against part of the turning wheel and slow it down with friction. Brake drums in a car work in similar way, but they press against the whole wheel.

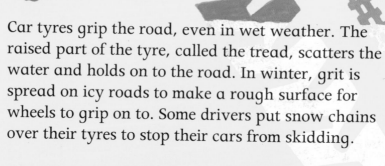

Car tyres grip the road, even in wet weather. The raised part of the tyre, called the tread, scatters the water and holds on to the road. In winter, grit is spread on icy roads to make a rough surface for wheels to grip on to. Some drivers put snow chains over their tyres to stop their cars from skidding.

If our feet move too quickly for the rest of our body, we fall over. This can happen on a slippery floor or on ice. On the bottom of shoes, rubber soles, thick tread, spikes and studs help to keep us upright.

Parachutes

Parachutists falling through the air need to slow down to break their fall. As a parachutist falls from the sky, gravity pulls them downwards; at the same time, some air is squashed inside the parachute and presses upwards. This makes the parachute drift slowly to the ground.

Something to try

Make your own parachutes

You will need: squares of different fabric cut to the same size, some string, equal size rolls of plasticine, scissors, stopwatch, some friends.

Cut four pieces of string to the same length. Stick one end of each length of string into the ball of plasticine. Tie the other ends of each piece of string to each of the four corners of the square. Make the other parachutes in the same way. Stand with the parachutes at the same height and drop them at the same time. Ask a friend to record how long each parachute takes to fall to the ground. Which parachute hits the ground first?

P.S. Make some parachutes out of circles of material. What happens?

21

Streamlining

Today, cars travel much faster than the cars of the 1920s. They have better engines and most are streamlined in shape, which means air passes easily over their smooth bodies, making very little air resistance. The shape of a new car is tested in a wind-tunnel. Smoky air is blown over the car and the patterns in the smoke show how the car will cut through the air as it moves along.

Rockets and aircraft are slim and sleek in shape, and, in the water, the fastest speed boats have smooth shiny hulls.

See which shapes dive the best

SAINT BENEDICT SCHOOL
DUFFIELD ROAD
DERBY DE22 1JD

You will need: a tall clear jug or cylinder, such as a spaghetti jar, plasticine.

Divide the plasticine into pieces of the same size and make each one into a different shape. Make shapes which you think will move quickly down the container and others which will sink slowly. Which of your shapes reached the bottom first? Did you guess correctly?

23

Moving pictures

If you see two slightly different pictures, very quickly one after the other, you may not notice that you have seen two pictures. Instead you see one picture which appears to move. When you are shown twelve pictures per second, you will see them as separate pictures, but if you see the pictures faster than this, you see moving pictures. Cinema films show you twenty-four photographs, or frames, per second.

Something to try

Make your own flicker book

You will need: a small notebook and a pencil.

On each page of the notebook, draw one of the pictures in this sequence. Each picture is slightly different from the one before. Make sure you draw only on the right-hand side of the page. Hold the notebook in one hand and flick the pages with your thumb on your other hand. You can watch the pictures start to move.

Try to draw your own sequence of pictures. Keep the pictures simple. Try drawing a match-stick person dancing or bouncing a ball.

24

The speed of light

Light from the Sun travels through space to Earth at a speed of 300 million metres per second. At this speed you could travel round the Earth eight times in one second. It takes eight minutes for the light from the Sun to reach us. A racing car travelling non-stop at top speed would take one hundred years to cover the same distance.

Light travels through water and glass more slowly than it does through air. When light rays travel from air into water, they bend at the surface. This is called refraction.

Something to try

See a straight pencil bend

Put some pencils in a glass of water. When you look at them they appear bent because light from the pencils is refracted, but when you lift them out of the water they are straight.

The speed of sound

Sound travels through air more slowly than light. During a storm, you may have noticed that you see lightning before you hear thunder. Lightning and thunder happen at the same time, but we see lightning almost immediately because light travels faster than sound. The sound waves from the thunder take longer to reach our ears.

To find out how far away a storm is, count the number of seconds between the lightning flash and the sound of thunder. Divide your answer by three and this is the storm's approximate distance from you in kilometres. The further away the storm is, the longer it will take for the sound of thunder to reach you.

An echo is a sound which bounces back so you can hear it again. When you shout at a rock face or a wall some distance away, you can sometimes hear an echo. A short time passes before you hear the echo because the sound waves travel at about 330 metres per second.

Measure the speed of sound

You will need: two spoons, a wall, stopwatch, the help of a friend.

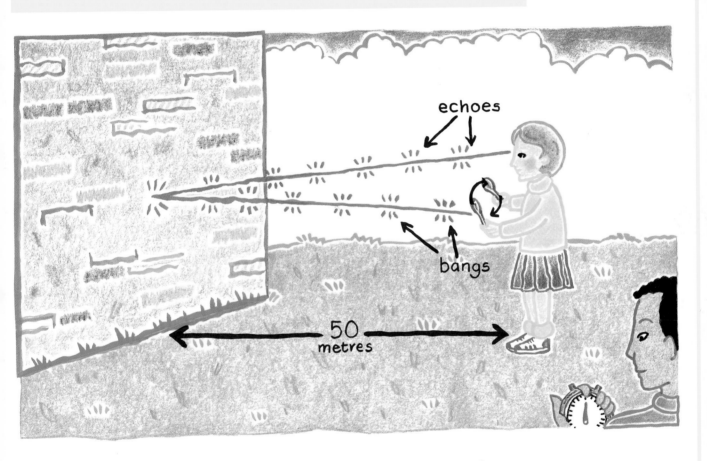

Stand 50 metres from a large wall. Bang two metal spoons together and wait for the echo. As soon as you hear the echo, bang the spoons again. Try to bang in an even rhythm, bang, echo, bang, echo. Ask a friend to time 100 of your bangs with a stopwatch. Between each bang, sound travels to and from the wall so it travels 100 metres. After 100 bangs the sound has travelled 100×100 metres (10,000 metres). Speed is the distance covered in a certain time, so if you divide 10,000 by the time it took you to make 100 bangs, you will have the approximate speed of sound.

Speed of life

As technology has advanced, so has the speed at which we do things. In medieval times, a journey of a few hundred miles could take several weeks to make on foot and on horseback. In the eighteenth century, horse-drawn carriages could travel the same distance in several days. In the nineteenth century, steam locomotives were invented. This picture shows George Stephenson's locomotive, called The Rocket. Today, high-speed trains can travel at over 160 kilometres per hour.

GEO. STEPHENSON'S ROCKET, 1829.

In medieval times, scrolls and books were hand-written and took years to produce. By the fifteenth century, the first European mechanical printing press had been invented and books could be printed in a few weeks. Today, millions of newspapers with up-to-date information can be prepared and printed overnight.

How many inventions can you think of that have speeded up our way of life?

Important events

3000 BC	In Mesopotamia, solid wheels joined to an axle were being used.
1750 BC	In Egypt, spoked wheels were being used.
1000 BC	In Europe, wooden ball bearings were used to help wheels turn more easily.
776 BC	The first Olympic Games were held in Athens.

490 BC — An athlete ran 40 kilometres from Marathon to Athens. The long-distance sporting race, the marathon, is named after this event.

800–950 — Viking invaders settle in Britain.

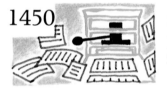

1450 — In Germany, Johannes Gutenberg invented the printing press. He was able to produce 300 printed pages each day. In Europe, printed books gradually replaced hand-written books.

1492 — Columbus's voyage west in search of the Spice Islands.

1732 — Henri Pitot invented the Pitot tube which measured water pressure. Later, the tube was adapted to measure air pressure. Today, the Pitot tube is used to help measure the speed of aircraft.

1832 — One of the first methods of producing moving pictures was invented.

1837–1901 — Queen Victoria's reign.

1930 — Amy Johnson flew from England to Australia in 19 days. She was the first woman to make the flight alone.

1939–1945 — Second World War.

1954 — Roger Bannister ran the first four-minute mile.

1983 — Richard Noble set a new land speed record of 1109.467 kilometres per hour in his rocket driven car 'Thrust 2'.

More things to do

SAINT BENEDICT SCHOOL
DUFFIELD ROAD
DERBY DE22 1JD

1 Page 5 Five minutes is one twelfth of an hour. If you take the number of metres that you walk in 5 minutes and multiply it by 12, you will find the number of metres that you would walk in one hour. If you divide this number by 1,000, you will find the number of kilometres that you would walk in one hour.

2 The fastest bird is the peregrine falcon which can dive at speeds of up to 350 kilometres per hour. The fastest marine mammal is the killer whale which can swim at 30 knots or 55 kilometres per hour. Racehorses can run at speeds of 65 kilometres per hour. Make a pictorial chart of the world's fastest animals.

3 Find out who holds the world record for the 100 metre sprint. If this athlete could keep up this speed for longer, approximately how long would it take him or her to cover a distance of 1 kilometre?

4 Look out for traffic signs which show the speed limit. How fast are cars allowed to travel on a motorway?

5 Find out about the land speed record. Often, attempts at the land speed record are made in the Nevada Desert in the United States. Try to find out why.

6 When a rocket is fired into space, it must travel at great speed to escape from the pull of Earth's gravity. Satellites orbiting in space have to travel at a speed of about 8 kilometres per hour to stay up in space. Find out about satellites that supply information on the weather and help with communications around the world.

7 In water, sound travels four times faster than it does in air. At sea, some ships have instruments which use sound waves to gauge the depth of the sea and to discover shoals of fish and submarines beneath them. A pulse of sound travels down through the water and is bounced back to the ship. The time difference between sending the pulse of sound and hearing the echo shows how far away an object is. This system is called SONAR, which stands for Sound Navigation And Ranging.

8 Read Aesop's fable about the tortoise and the hare. Why was the speedy hare beaten by the plodding tortoise?

9 Do you know the sayings 'More haste, less speed' and 'No sooner said than done'? What do they mean? Can you think of any other sayings about speed?

DERBY DE22 1JD

Index

First published 1992
A & C Black (Publishers) Limited
35 Bedford Row, London WC1R 4JH

ISBN 0–7136–3546 0

© 1992 A & C Black
  (Publishers) Limited

A CIP catalogue record for this book is available from the British Library.

Acknowledgements
Photographs by Chris Fairclough, except for: p2 Paul Ridsdale CFCL; p3 (b), p6, p10, p11 (b), p16 (t), p20, p28 (b), p29 (1) CFCL; p4 (t) John Cox CFCL; p4 (b) Michael Holford; p5 (t) Bruce Coleman; p7 Allsport; p8 National Maritime Museum; p17 Mike Morton CFCL; p21 (1) John Davies CFCL; p22 Ford Motor Company; p26 Jon Arnold CFCL; 28 (t) Mary Evans Picture Library; p29 (r) The Hulton Picture Company; main cover photo Graham Taylor, CFCL.

The author and publisher would like to thank the staff and pupils of Thornhill Primary School, and Rose Griffiths and Alistair Ross for their help and advice.

Apart from any fair dealing for the purposes of research or private study, or criticism or review, as permitted under the Copyright, Designs and Patents Act, 1988, this publication may be reproduced, stored or transmitted, in any form or by any means, only with the prior permission in writing of the publishers, or in the case of reprographic reproduction in accordance with the terms of licences issued by the Copyright Licensing Agency. Inquiries concerning reproduction outside those terms should be sent to the publishers at the above named address.

Filmset by August Filmsetting, Haydock, St Helens
Printed in Belgium by Proost International Book Production

SAINT BENEDICT SCHOOL
DUFFIELD ROAD
DERBY DE22 1JD